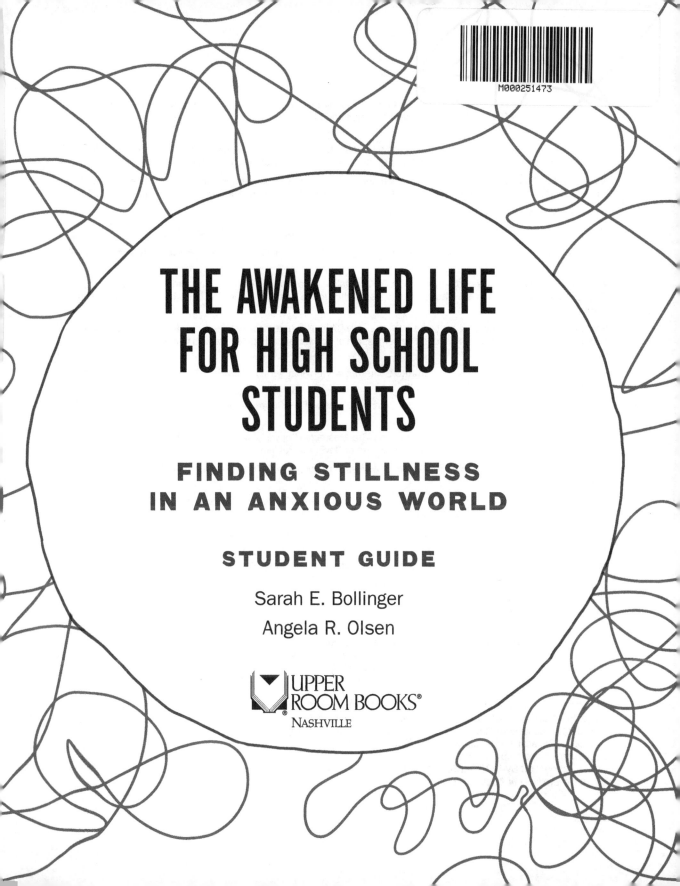

THE AWAKENED LIFE FOR HIGH SCHOOL STUDENTS

FINDING STILLNESS IN AN ANXIOUS WORLD

STUDENT GUIDE

Sarah E. Bollinger

Angela R. Olsen

UPPER ROOM BOOKS®
NASHVILLE

Library of Congress Cataloging-in-Publication Data
Names: Bollinger, Sarah E., author. | Olsen, Angela R., author.
Title: The awakened life for high school students : finding stillness in an
   anxious world : student guide / Sarah E. Bollinger, Angela R. Olsen.
Description: Nashville, TN : Upper Room Books, [2020] | Includes
   bibliographical references.
Identifiers: LCCN 2020004375 | ISBN 9780835819398 (paperback)
Subjects: LCSH: High school students—Religious life. | High school
   students—Conduct of life. | Spiritual formation—Christianity. | Prayer
   groups—Christianity. | Meditation—Christianity. | Spiritual
   journals—Authorship.
Classification: LCC BV4531.3 .B65 2020 | DDC 248.8/3—dc23
LC record available at *https://lccn.loc.gov/2020004375*

Wake me up, God! Help me to live more fully in my day-to-day life. Let me savor and find deep satisfaction in the simple moments, receiving each as a miraculous gift from you.

MADELINE BONNER, 19, GEORGIA
(devozine)

CONTENTS

Welcome 7

Getting Started 9

Week 1. Introduction to the Awakened Life 11

Week 2. Connecting to Self: Noticing Thoughts 23

Week 3. Connecting to Self: Being Present in the Body 35

Week 4. Connecting to Others: Working Through Loneliness 49

Week 5. Connecting to Others: Working Through Shame 63

Week 6. Connecting to Creation: Experiencing Awe of Nature 79

Week 7. Connecting to Creation: Sharing a Meal of Intention 91

Week 8. Closing: Awakening to Joy 101

Notes 109

[Jesus said,] "I came that they may have life, and have it abundantly."

JOHN 10:10

WELCOME

Wake up! This is not your typical Bible study. This is an invitation to awaken to life. Too many of us are overwhelmed by anxiety, depression, worry, loneliness, and fear. Stressed and distracted, we miss so much of what makes life wonderful. We believe there is an alternative.

Within these pages, faith, practice, and science come together. We share the science behind the ways mindfulness and spiritual practices can reduce anxiety, worry, and depression. We explore practices of prayerful meditation that allow us to calm our minds, to slow down amid the pressures of life, and to find stillness in an anxious world. In this stillness, we can be present to the grace and love of God—and there, we can find wholeness and joy.

Daily spiritual practices open us to the abundant life God offers each of us. An abundant life is not one free of pain and worry but rather one rich in the beauty of all life has to offer—sadness *and* joy, seriousness *and* celebration, the ordinary *and* the transformational. Over the course of the next eight weeks, we invite you to explore new ways to get the most out of each moment and to see what God is doing in you, in your relationships, and in the world around you. We hope the practices you adopt and the insights you gain about yourself each week will bring you closer to God, help you build strength to face life's struggles, and awaken you to the joy of a more abundant life.

Your sisters,

Sarah & Angie

GETTING STARTED

The Awakened Life for High School Students is an eight-week study that provides tools and practices to empower you to live a more abundant life. This Student Guide will be your companion during this study, walking you through the spiritual practices and providing space for daily reflection. This guide also offers relevant research, discussion questions, activity instructions, and journal prompts for writing and drawing. Audio tracks and video clips can be accessed on the accompanying website, UpperRoomBooks.com/TheAwakenedLife. Here are the topics you will explore each week:

Week 1. Introduction to the Awakened Life

Week 2. Connecting to Self: Noticing Thoughts

Week 3. Connecting to Self: Being Present in the Body

Week 4. Connecting to Others: Working Through Loneliness

Week 5. Connecting to Others: Working Through Shame

Week 6. Connecting to Creation: Experiencing Awe of Nature

Week 7. Connecting to Creation: Sharing a Meal of Intention

Week 8. Closing: Awakening to Joy

Each week's session will include the following five sections:

 Awake: Each week will begin with an **introductory section**. This is your call to wake up, join in, and participate in exploring new practices and possibilities.

 Aware: This section creates awareness by revealing **scientific studies and real-life examples** that illustrate how living an anxious life can affect the body, mind, and spirit.

Alive: This section includes **journal prompts and group exercises** that allow you to engage actively with each session's topic and the ways it relates to your own life. These activities can deepen your connection to God, others, and nature.

 Abide: This section provides **spiritual practices** handed down through the generations. These grace-filled practices help us to experience God's presence and unconditional love for us.

 Arise: This section offers a **summary** of the session and reviews the assignments to be completed between sessions.

We know you are busy with homework and all kinds of activities. Still, we encourage you to use these practices daily. Keep in mind that these spiritual practices and mindfulness techniques can bring calm and clarity as you use them. Here are some tips:

- **Set an alarm** for the same time every day to remind you to practice.

- **Write or draw**. Reflect on your practice as part of your daily routine. Blank space and prompts are provided in this Student Guide. Or you can use a personal journal or sketch pad.

- **Extend compassion to yourself.** Everyone feels a little awkward when they first try these practices, but your life will be better if you put in the effort.

At the end of the eight weeks, we pray these practices will help you to find stillness in God's presence, to remind you of the beauty life offers, and to cultivate joy and hope for years to come. God is working in and through you right now! We hope you stay awake and connected and you live each moment fully.

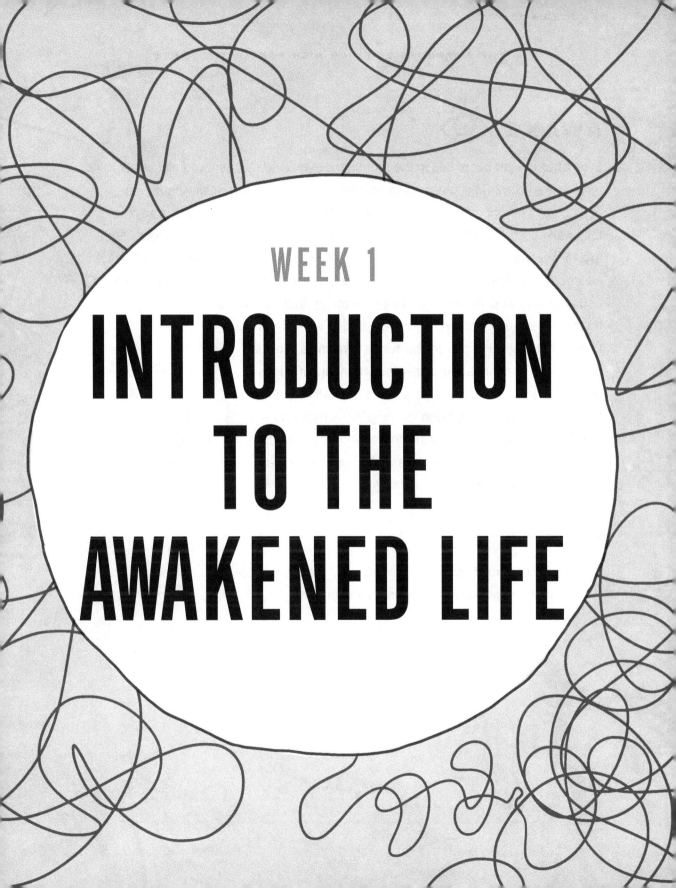

WEEK 1

INTRODUCTION TO THE AWAKENED LIFE

AWAKE

Even after you get out of bed in the morning, do you ever feel as if you sleepwalk through your day? Do your thoughts wander so much that you miss what is happening right in front of you? For the next eight weeks, we will be practicing ways to fully wake up to our lives. The biblical term *abundant life* can help us understand what it means to be awake and fully alive. *Abundance* describes a state of being connected, healthy, and whole. Unfortunately, many of us miss out on this awakened and abundant life. We focus on negative things that happened in the past, we are distracted by our screens, or we worry about things that might happen in the future. We miss the fullness and joy that are at our fingertips. Abundant life does not mean life without struggle or pain but rather a life deeply connected to what God is doing in the moment—in us, in our relationships with others, and in the world around us. When living an abundant life, hope and joy are accessible, even in the midst of struggle.

> **I am about to do a new thing; now it springs forth, do you not perceive it?**
> **ISAIAH 43:19**

Reflection

- Describe a moment in your life when you felt fully present and awake to something wonderful that was happening.

AWARE

THE WHY

Did you know that one in five teens live with a mental illness?[1] High school can be stressful; students can feel pressure to make good grades, to get into college or decide what to do after graduation, and to meet the expectations of parents, teachers, and friends.[2] Many teens also struggle with depression, anxiety, and other mental health issues. Anxiety and depression may be part of your life as well. If so, hear this clearly: You are not alone. You do not have to feel ashamed. There is hope.

Fortunately, a number of strategies are available to help us build strength and resiliency. Resiliency describes our ability to "bounce back" after a difficult or traumatic experience. Mindfulness, spiritual practices, healthy relationships, and time in nature have all been scientifically proven to improve mental health. During our time together, we will explore a number of mindfulness and spiritual practices. These practices invite us to take one moment at a time and to live fully in the present. We will build an awakened life together through these simple, life-giving practices.

> Teens are stressed to the max. Even when we relax, our to-do lists are racing through our minds. Our culture feeds on speed, and impatience thrives on minutes wasted. How can we find a moment of silence in the monotonous, never-pausing noise of life?
>
> **KATIE SWEENEY, 19, GEORGIA**
> **(devozine)**

NOTE: Mindfulness and spiritual practices are useful tools, but they do not replace medicine and counseling. If you are struggling with anxiety or depression, talk to your group leader, pastor, or an adult you trust about how you are feeling, and ask for help.

INTRO TO MEDITATION

Awakening to God working in and through you in the present moment takes practice. During meditation exercises, you will take time to pause and be present, to listen to your breathing, and to notice, without judgment, what is going on in your mind and body. If meditative prayer and mindfulness are not already part of your daily life, it might be difficult for you, initially, to sit in silence; and that's OK. Be kind to yourself as you learn and grow in this practice.

Listen > *Week 1: Awareness Meditation*

To practice the awareness meditation, listen to the audio track "Week 1: Awareness Meditation" at UpperRoomBooks.com/TheAwakenedLife, and follow the instructions.

Prayer

God, help me to be fully present and thankful for each breath. Amen.

Reflection

- How did you feel while practicing this meditation?
- What are your initial reactions to this practice?

Being still with God is the healing and restoration I need in the midst of a busy life.
HANNAH BEAVEN, 16, INDIANA
(devozine)

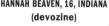

ALIVE

Feel free to respond to these journal prompts with whatever comes to mind. You can write or draw without judgment. Don't worry about editing or erasing. Give yourself time to brainstorm without filtering your thoughts.

JOURNAL

Describe a time when you felt peaceful, connected, and whole in mind, body, and spirit. What contributed to your feeling this way?

What pressures, demands, or expectations make your life stressful? What keeps you from feeling peaceful, connected, and whole?

Describe a particularly difficult or stressful situation you have faced this year. How did you respond to that situation?

When you are faced with challenges, what gives you resiliency? What helps you to "bounce back"?

When have you felt closest to God? How did that experience affect you?

ABIDE

LECTIO DIVINA

This week's spiritual practice is an ancient Christian practice called *lectio divina,* which means "divine reading." *Lectio divina* includes focused reading, meditation, and prayer. This practice begins with a prayer inviting the Holy Spirit to reveal something to you through the experience.

Find a quiet place to spend time with God. Then, choose a scripture or poem from the following list. You might wish to use the same scripture or poem each day to deepen your understanding and experience of the text, but you also can use a different text each day.

- John 10:10

- Psalm 46:10

- Psalm 139:13-14

- Matthew 11:28

- Excerpt from Hafiz, "Awake Awhile":

  Awake, my dear.
  Be kind to your sleeping heart.
  Take it out into the vast fields of Light
  And let it breathe.[3]

- Excerpt from John O'Donohue, "The Question Holds the Lantern":

  Once you start to awaken, no one can ever claim you again for the old patterns.
  . . . You want your God to be wild and to call you to where your destiny awaits.[4]

Once you have chosen your text, find a comfortable position. Then, ask God to focus your thoughts and to reveal to you something you need to hear as you practice *lectio divina*. Then, read through the selected scripture or poem excerpt three times. The first time, read it slowly in your mind. The second time, read it slowly out loud. The third time, read it again in your mind, noting which word or words stand out to you. Then, spend some quiet time listening for God's still small voice, noting further what the passage says to you. Pay attention to the way God invites you to care for your physical, mental, emotional, and spiritual health.

Each time you practice *lectio divina* this week, log a new entry in your daily practice journal at the end of Week 1. Note any thoughts or feelings that emerged during the practice. Also, include what you noticed about your body: perhaps your shoulders were tense, you felt a knot in your stomach, or your breathing grew more relaxed. You may capture these observations with words or doodles. Remember that the purpose of the practice journal is to increase your awareness; there is no wrong answer.

ARISE

Today you learned about the importance of being awake, aware, and alive in the moment. Next week, you will dig into the incredibly and uniquely beautiful person God has created you to be. Before the group meets again, it's important to practice what you have learned. To notice lasting change, regular practice is key.

> "Be still, and know that I am God!"
> PSALM 46:10

PRACTICE PARTNERS

Commitment to daily practices will be an important part of this study. To help you honor that commitment, you will have a practice partner. The two of you will check in with each other during the week and encourage each other to practice the spiritual disciplines and mindfulness exercises you are learning. The information below will help you connect with your practice partner throughout the next seven weeks.

Name: _____

Phone number: _____

Email address: _____

HOME PRACTICES FOR WEEK 1

1. Try the Abide spiritual practice (*lectio divina*) every day. You might want to try practicing at the same time each day.

2. Keep track of your reactions and insights in the practice journal section that begins on page 20. For example, on Day 1, enter the date you practiced and the practice: "*lectio divina.*" Then, record anything you notice about your thoughts, emotions, and physical body. Keep in mind that there is no wrong answer.

3. Check in with your partner at least twice this week. If you want to try practicing *lectio divina* together, you can take turns reading aloud the scripture or quote you choose.

CLOSING BLESSING

We will end each group session with this blessing. You also might want to close your daily practice times or your practice partner conversations with this affirmation of all that God is awakening in you.

We are awakening to abundant life.

We are becoming aware of our worth and belonging.

We are coming alive to our senses, thoughts, and emotions.

We are abiding in the love and grace of God.

We arise now to live a life as connected, whole people.

Therefore encourage one another and build up each other, as indeed you are doing.
1 THESSALONIANS 5:11

DAILY PRACTICE JOURNAL

DAY 1

Date: Practice:

What do you notice about your thoughts, emotions, and physical body?

DAY 2

Date: Practice:

What do you notice about your thoughts, emotions, and physical body?

DAY 3

Date: Practice:

What do you notice about your thoughts, emotions, and physical body?

DAY 4

Date: Practice:

What do you notice about your thoughts, emotions, and physical body?

DAY 5

Date: Practice:

What do you notice about your thoughts, emotions, and physical body?

DAY 6

Date: Practice:

What do you notice about your thoughts, emotions, and physical body?

DAY 7

Date: Practice:

What do you notice about your thoughts, emotions, and physical body?

WEEK 2

CONNECTING TO SELF

NOTICING
THOUGHTS

AWAKE 👁

How cool is the mind—it keeps us alive! Our minds do everything from signaling our breathing to processing the words we are reading. We are designed to have our minds wander, to scan the horizon for danger, and to learn new things. It's OK for our minds to be busy, but sometimes our busy minds can get the best of us. Instead of making us more aware of our surroundings, our anxious and negative thoughts can spiral and take us completely out of the moment. The truth is that we are more than our thoughts. Thoughts can be helpful, but ultimately, our thoughts change from day to day, or even from moment to moment. When we think about past regrets or worry about the future, we miss the present moment—the only moment in which we truly can be alive. Yet, we can train our minds in the same way that we train the muscles in our bodies. With training, we can notice our thoughts without allowing them to rob us of our present-moment awareness. With training, we can find amazing freedom to focus on what is truly important to us.

AWARENESS MEDITATION

Listen > *Week 2: Awareness Meditation*

To practice the awareness meditation, listen to the audio track "Week 2: Awareness Meditation" at UpperRoomBooks.com/TheAwakenedLife, and follow the instructions.

> Maybe silence and stillness aren't defined by volume or environment; maybe they are a mindset. Turning off the noise and closing the door may be only half the battle. We may also need to quiet our minds.
>
> **AMELIA NGUYEN, 15, NEW YORK**
> **(devozine)**

Prayer

God, help me to notice my own thoughts and to be thankful for my mind. Amen.

Reflection

- What thoughts did you notice during the meditation?
- What were your reactions to those thoughts?

AWARE

THE WHY

Being aware of our thoughts is important to our mental, physical, and spiritual health. Most people's minds wander; in fact, we spend almost half of our waking hours thinking about something other than what we are doing.[1] When our minds wander, we are no longer in the present moment. This habit can make us feel disconnected and unhappy.

Thoughts can be distracting and overwhelming; but ultimately, thoughts are just thoughts. They are real but not always true. In other words, thoughts are not always facts. Noticing and naming thought patterns, specifically the negative thought patterns that grab hold of our minds, is key to minimizing their power over our lives.

Negative Thought Patterns

Here are some examples of negative thought patterns that you may experience in your life:[2]

- **Catastrophizing**—jumping to the worst-case scenario
- **Mind-Reading**—assuming what others are thinking, without knowing their real thoughts
- **The "Shoulds"**—feeling as if you need to do something because of some unwritten rule
- **Blaming**—holding others responsible for your own pain and suffering
- **The Comparison Trap**—measuring yourself against your peers (often on social media)
- **FOMO (Fear of Missing Out)**—wanting to be constantly connected

Group Activity

Read the following example and consider what negative thought patterns are at work in this scenario.

> Lauren was walking to class yesterday and saw her friend Rachel down
> the hall. They hadn't seen each other in several days, and Lauren was

excited to connect. Lauren looked up and waved, but Rachel kept her head down, walking quickly to her next class. Immediately, Lauren started thinking about worst-case scenarios: *Is Rachel mad at me? Why didn't she come over to talk to me—or at least wave back? What happened when I was with her last? Maybe I said something that offended her, or maybe she's just being a jerk.* Lauren walked on to class but couldn't stop thinking about how Rachel had acted. This interaction influenced her mood for the rest of the afternoon, making her crabby and anxious.

Discussion

After you have read the scenario, discuss these questions with your group.

- With which negative thought patterns does Lauren struggle?
- What could Lauren do to bring awareness to these negative thought patterns?

Thoughts and beliefs are navigational maps that are not inherently true.
TARA BRACH

ALIVE

JOURNAL

Now that you are aware of some of these negative thought patterns, take a few moments to consider any of these patterns you have experienced. As you did last week, allow yourself time to write or draw without editing or erasing.

Which of these negative thought patterns have you experienced? Make a list, and then circle the patterns you experience most often.

Describe a time when you have experienced one of these negative thought patterns.

What situations can cause these types of thoughts in you? How do you typically respond when you start having negative thoughts?

Describe a time when you noticed a friend or family member using one of these negative thought patterns. What did they do or say? How did you respond?

ABOUT SELF-COMPASSION

In the greatest commandment in the New Testament, Jesus instructs us to love God with our whole being and to love our neighbor as ourselves. Yet all too often, loving ourselves and showing ourselves compassion is not something we practice. Instead, when we take time to notice our own thoughts, we often judge them or try to change them.

Practicing self-compassion is crucial to mental and spiritual health. According to psychologist Kristin Neff, "Self-compassion is treating yourself with the same kindness, care, and concern you show a loved one."[3] Self-compassion does not mean hiding our flaws or ignoring our mistakes. Flaws and mistakes are what make us human! Neff suggests that we remind ourselves, "'I'm an imperfect human living an imperfect life.'"[4] When we practice self-compassion, we practice loving and forgiving ourselves the way that God loves and forgives us.

Reflection

- How might you show kindness and compassion to yourself when you recognize your own negative thought patterns? How can you greet negative thoughts with compassion and curiosity rather than judgment and fear?

- In what ways have you shown (or might you show) kindness and compassion to a friend or family member whom you have seen engaging in negative thought patterns?

"Teacher, which commandment in the law is the greatest?" He said to him, "'You shall love the Lord your God with all your heart, and with all your soul, and with all your mind.' This is the greatest and first commandment. And a second is like it: 'You shall love your neighbor as yourself.'"

MATTHEW 22:36-39

ABIDE

AWARENESS MEDITATION WITH COMPASSION

A mantra is a short statement that you can repeat to yourself when you notice negative thoughts drawing you away from the present moment. Create a mantra that reminds you to practice self-compassion. You can write it in the blank circle here:

As we learn to quiet our minds and become more aware of our thoughts, we remember that distractions and negative thought patterns are a part of life. Everyone has them. Practicing self-compassion here means letting go of judgment. Instead of trying to change these thoughts, we can observe them and move on. Try the awareness meditation again using the mantra you created. As before, you may use the audio track "Week 2: Awareness Meditation" at UpperRoomBooks.com/TheAwakenedLife.

Prayer

God, help me to notice my own thoughts, to be thankful for my mind, and to love myself as you love me. Amen.

Reflection

- How did you extend compassion to yourself during this meditation?
- How did this experience with the awareness meditation differ from the first?

Talk to yourself the way you'd talk to someone you love.
BRENÉ BROWN

ARISE

Today, you began to awaken to your mind and learned about the importance of self-compassion. Use the home practices this week to begin to get curious about how your mind works.

HOME PRACTICES FOR WEEK 2

1. Practice each day your awareness meditation *with compassion*. Start with three minutes. If that feels comfortable, challenge yourself the next day by adding a minute.

2. Keep track of your observations in the practice journal area that follows. For example, on Day 1, enter the date you practiced and the practice: "awareness meditation." Then, record anything you notice about your thoughts, emotions, and physical body. Keep in mind that there is no wrong answer.

3. Check in with your practice partner at least twice this week.

CLOSING BLESSING

We are awakening to abundant life.

We are becoming aware of our worth and belonging.

We are coming alive to our senses, thoughts, and emotions.

We are abiding in the love and grace of God.

We arise now to live a life as connected, whole people.

DAILY PRACTICE JOURNAL

DAY 1

Date: Practice:

What do you notice about your thoughts, emotions, and physical body?

DAY 2

Date: Practice:

What do you notice about your thoughts, emotions, and physical body?

DAY 3

Date: Practice:

What do you notice about your thoughts, emotions, and physical body?

DAY 4

Date: Practice:

What do you notice about your thoughts, emotions, and physical body?

DAY 5

Date: Practice:

What do you notice about your thoughts, emotions, and physical body?

DAY 6

Date: Practice:

What do you notice about your thoughts, emotions, and physical body?

DAY 7

Date: Practice:

What do you notice about your thoughts, emotions, and physical body?

WEEK 3

CONNECTING TO SELF

BEING PRESENT IN THE BODY

AWAKE

Have you ever taken time to marvel at the miracle of your own body? Your eyes perceive the smile of a friend, funny cat videos, and the majesty of the mountains. Your nose breathes in the smell of bread baking and the fragrance of a budding flower. Your ears soak in your own voice speaking your truth, your joyful singing in your car, and the precious moment when you hear the words "I love you." Your mouth opens to the sweetness of honey and the pleasure of macaroni and cheese. Your skin intimately connects you to the delight of goose bump-inducing music, the power of clicking on a text message, and the shelter of a hug.

Not only does your body make all these memorable experiences possible; it also allows you to connect with your mind and your soul. This mind, body, soul connection is crucial to wholeness. Your body signals you when you are hungry, tired, anxious, hurt, or sad. If you do not pay attention to these signals, your body becomes sluggish and cannot function properly. This disconnect can lead to spiraling thoughts that make it easier to forget that you are a precious child of God, designed with all the tools necessary to live abundantly. God's breath is in you, and you are "fearfully and wonderfully made" (Ps. 139:14). You were created with the ability to know when you need to rest, nourish, heal, protect, and soothe your body. This week, you will focus on paying attention to what your body reveals to you about healthy ways to live. Again, this takes practice, but it is worth the effort.

> O taste and see that the LORD is good.
> PSALM 34:8

AWARE

THE WHY

For some of us, staying "in the now," being present to all that is happening in the moment, is seemingly impossible. Instead, we numb ourselves: We binge-watch videos or sports, gossip with friends, or log on to social media. Sometimes, we actively seek ways to avoid the present—when we are feeling anxious or lonely, procrastinating on homework, or dreading a tough conversation with a friend. Other times, we numb ourselves without realizing we are doing it; we reach for our smartphones to connect or scroll through social media without considering what "real-life" moments we might be missing.

> Our bodies are incredible. . . . When I pause to think about God creating our hearts to pump 70 times a minute and our lungs to inhale and exhale 12 to 20 times a minute, I realize that my life is an amazing gift. I am a miracle, and so are you.
>
> **REBEKAH VIJAY, 17, PENNSYLVANIA**
> **(devozine)**

Smartphone technology has many benefits; our smartphones have the potential to keep us connected to people and give us access to information and entertainment. However, many people report that phone use often isolates them from others as well as from what is happening in and around them. In a *Psychology Today* article, a student shares his experience at dinner with some friends:

> Speaking of being tethered and isolating myself, just a few nights ago I went out to eat with my friends, and half the time we were at the restaurant I was constantly checking my phone; in fact I was too busy checking my own to even notice if anyone else had been looking at theirs. For some parts of the conversation I just gave short replies or nods to the conversation because I was missing what was actually being said. Even watching this video for class, I had to stop and rewind a few times because I found myself getting distracted by my phone.[1]

Phone use can numb our senses. It can take us out of the present moment, causing us to miss out on what is happening around and in us. Avoiding the present has serious consequences for our bodies. Avoidance can make us anxious, and in turn, we carry this stress knowingly and unknowingly in our bodies.

Our bodies give us the best information about what is happening inside us right now; they connect us to the present. Instead of numbing and shutting out these messages, we can learn to sit with our own thoughts and feelings and to experience how they affect our bodies. The body signals its needs if we listen to it. For instance, our stomach growls when we are hungry, and our eyes get heavy when we are tired. Listening to these signals and nourishing and taking care of our bodies can improve our physical, mental, and emotional health.

JOURNAL

Describe a time when you numbed yourself to avoid a situation. How did you "numb out"—perhaps by binge-watching Netflix or scrolling through social media? What were you avoiding—maybe a tough conversation or uncomfortable feelings (anxiety, loneliness, or guilt)? What did you miss out on? How did it affect your body?

Describe a time when you did not listen to your body's signals. How did your body signal its needs? What happened when you ignored this signal? (Maybe you gave in to a negative thought pattern, or you snapped at your friend.) What do you remember about your thoughts, emotions, and physical response? If you could go back and pay attention to your body cues, how do you think the experience would be different?

ALIVE

MOVEMENT EXERCISES

Use these exercises to become more present to your body.

Exercise 1

Clench your fists as tightly as you can, and hold them closed for fifteen seconds; then, unclench them. Notice what you feel in your hands.

- Describe the feeling.

- What sensations are you experiencing? Tingling? warmth? tension? other?

Now, smile for fifteen seconds; then, relax your face.

- Describe the feeling.

- How is this feeling different from what you felt after clenching your fists?

Exercise 2

Pick one of the scenarios that follow. Take a few moments to think about how you would react. What might happen in your mind and body if this scenario occurred? How would you feel? What would you think? How would your body respond in relation to your thoughts and feelings? Act out how you think your body might react.

- You ate a whole bag of chips or a pint of ice cream by yourself.

- You stayed up all night playing on your phone.

- You partied too hard on Friday and missed a test prep session the next morning.

- You canceled a get-together with a friend and stayed home instead to binge-watch videos.

- You failed a quiz.

Exercise 3

Adopt a pose of self-compassion. Here are some possibilities:

- Use a hand to gently cradle your face.

- Hug yourself.

- Place a comforting hand on your heart.

Take a selfie of your self-compassion pose. Then, text it to yourself along with a note of self-compassion and love. Anytime you feel anxious, look at this selfie and recall the words of self-compassion you sent to yourself.

ABIDE

BODY PRAYERS

We often think of prayer as words spoken aloud or silently in our own minds. But when we think of prayer only as words, we downplay the importance of our physical posture. Our bodies can communicate what we are thinking and feeling; conversely, physical movement can help to shape our thoughts and feelings. For example, sometimes when we are in a bad mood, going for a walk can help change our perspective. Similarly, what we might have trouble expressing through words can sometimes be better expressed through our physical postures. Prayerful movement and postures can open us to receive new insights and understanding; they also enable us to express ourselves beyond words and to communicate with God in deeper ways.

> When my name was called, I took my place on stage. As the music played, I danced from my heart. I wasn't dancing to win a competition. My dance was a prayer—a prayer that the world might be set on fire for God.
>
> **ELIZABETH MANN MCCHARGUE, 23, NORTH CAROLINE**
> **(devozine)**

To practice body prayer, you can choose between the following options:

OPTION 1: Prayer Postures

Postures of prayer have been used by monks and nuns for centuries. Some of these postures are described in the Bible; others have been adopted over time. Here are just a few:

Kneeling with head bowed and hands folded

Standing with arms stretched upward, palms up

Sitting with head facing upward and both hands clasped over the heart

Lying prostrate (face down) on the ground with arms outstretched, forming a cross with the body

Sitting cross-legged, with a straight back, hands on thigh, palms open

Reflection

- What other postures might communicate your thoughts and feelings to God?
- What new prayer postures might you add to this list?

OPTION 2: Body Movement

Body movement can also be a form of prayer. This body prayer option pairs a sequence of yoga poses with the words of Psalm 46:10-11.

"Be still, and know that I am God!

I am exalted among the nations,

I am exalted in the earth."

The LORD of hosts is with us;

the God of Jacob is our refuge.

Reflection

- What thoughts or emotions did you experience while adopting each pose?

- How do you usually pray? How does this experience compare?

Try to practice a body prayer each day during the week. You can use the prayer posture or body movement prayer that you practiced today; you can try a different body movement prayer (with yoga sequence) available at UpperRoomBooks.com/TheAwakenedLife; or you can create a new prayer each day by combining postures or poses.

ARISE

Today, you began to awaken to your physical body and became more aware of the ways you often avoid or ignore the sensory input your body provides.

HOME PRACTICE FOR WEEK 3

1. Try the Abide spiritual practice (body prayer) each day. You can repeat the body prayer from the session, try a new one available at UpperRoomBooks.com/TheAwakenedLife, or create your own by combining two or three prayer postures or yoga poses, perhaps to accompany a favorite scripture passage.

2. Keep track of your observations in the practice journal area that follows. For example, on Day 1, enter the date you practiced and the practice: "body prayer." Then, record anything you notice about your thoughts, emotions, and physical body. Keep in mind that there is no wrong answer.

3. Check in with your practice partner at least twice this week. You might want to create a body prayer sequence and practice it together.

CLOSING BLESSING

We are awakening to abundant life.

We are becoming aware of our worth and belonging.

We are coming alive to our senses, thoughts, and emotions.

We are abiding in the love and grace of God.

We arise now to live a life as connected, whole people.

DAILY PRACTICE JOURNAL

DAY 1

Date: Practice:

What do you notice about your thoughts, emotions, and physical body?

DAY 2

Date: Practice:

What do you notice about your thoughts, emotions, and physical body?

DAY 3

Date: Practice:

What do you notice about your thoughts, emotions, and physical body?

DAY 4

Date: Practice:

What do you notice about your thoughts, emotions, and physical body?

DAY 5

Date: Practice:

What do you notice about your thoughts, emotions, and physical body?

DAY 6

Date: Practice:

What do you notice about your thoughts, emotions, and physical body?

DAY 7

Date: Practice:

What do you notice about your thoughts, emotions, and physical body?

WEEK 4

CONNECTING TO OTHERS

WORKING
THROUGH
LONELINESS

AWAKE

Over the last three weeks, you began awakening to God's presence in your mind and body. By listening to your own thoughts and feelings, you are beginning to extend compassion to yourself. By quieting negative thoughts and diminishing the distractions, you are creating space to experience an awakened and abundant life. Hopefully, you are realizing or remembering that you are a beloved child of God who is held in grace. God's grace is the unconditional love and transforming power given freely to you and available in each moment.

The next step is connecting to other people. As you quiet your mind and extend compassion to yourself, you can begin to make space for others. As you recognize that you are a beloved child of God, you also realize that God's love extends to everyone. As you sense God working in and through you, you can celebrate the ways God is also working in and through other people. As you embrace your own worth, you can acknowledge the worth of others and build meaningful relationships.

LOVING-KINDNESS MEDITATION

We are created to be in relationship with one another. Being present with others, like being awake and present to ourselves, is a skill we develop over years. This week, we will practice loving-kindness meditation. We will begin by offering loving-kindness to ourselves, and then we will extend that loving-kindness to others.

Listen > *Week 4: Loving-Kindness Meditation 1*

To practice loving-kindness meditation, listen to the audio track "Week 4: Loving-Kindness Meditation 1" at UpperRoomBooks.com/TheAwakenedLife, and follow the instructions.

If we hate ourselves, we can never love others, for love is the gift of oneself. How will you make a gift of that which you hate?

WILLIAM SLOANE COFFIN

Prayer

God, help me to be fully present and thankful for the opportunity to share life with the people in this group. Amen.

Reflection

- How did you feel while participating in this practice?
- What do you need to let go of so that you can be fully present?

AWARE

THE WHY

Have you ever felt lonely in a crowded room? Have you ever felt lonely sitting with friends who are on their phones? Have you opened your phone to connect but wound up feeling more alone as you scrolled through social media? Loneliness does not necessarily mean *being* alone but *feeling* alone. Loneliness is a feeling of disconnection—a feeling that no one "gets" you or that you do not have the meaningful relationships you would like to have.

If you feel lonely, you are not the only one feeling that way. A recent study (BBC's *Loneliness Experiment*) found that levels of loneliness are highest among sixteen-to-twenty-four-year-olds. More than 40 percent of young people said they often feel lonely, compared to 27 percent of people over the age of seventy-five.[1] Four out of ten young people surveyed said they often felt misunderstood, sad, detached, and like they did not have anyone to talk with. Another study showed that

> I spent hours on the underground train system when I lived in London. While on their commute to various locations within the city, passengers would listen to music, read a book, or play on their phones. . . . We were each alone, living our individual lives. These people each had their own lives, fears, worries, and dreams that I knew nothing about; and they knew nothing about mine.
>
> **ELIZABETH A. HARTMANN, OHIO**
> (devozine)

the number of teens who feel lonely has increased over the past decade; in 2017, 39 per-cent of high school seniors said they often felt lonely, compared to 26 percent in 2012.[2]

If you feel lonely and disconnected, you can do something about it. Meaningful rela-tionships are beautiful and messy. They take effort, but they are worth the investment and lead to experiences of love, respect, and connection. Did you know science has proven that when individuals sing a song in a choir, the hearts of the singers begin to beat as one in rhythm with the music and with one another?[3] Interconnection is possible and real.

God, we need people to sit across the table from us at a coffee shop. We need people to wrap their arms around us when we experience disappointing news. We need people to see the truth in our eyes when we lie and say everything is OK. Help me to be a friend to someone else. Help me to cultivate authentic relationships. Amen.

TYNEA LEWIS, PENNSYLVANIA
(devozine)

ALIVE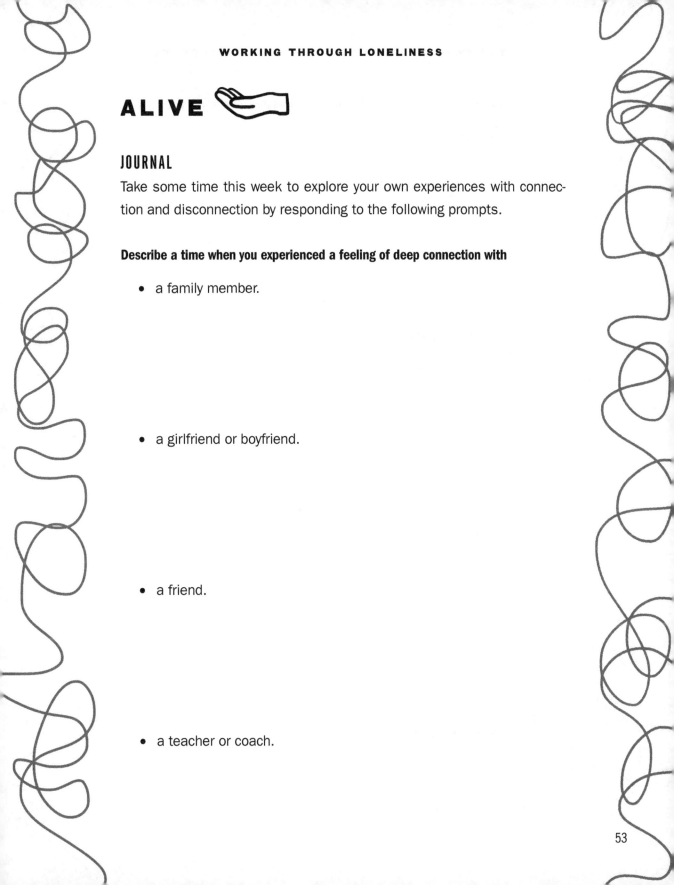

JOURNAL

Take some time this week to explore your own experiences with connection and disconnection by responding to the following prompts.

Describe a time when you experienced a feeling of deep connection with

- a family member.

- a girlfriend or boyfriend.

- a friend.

- a teacher or coach.

Describe a time when you experienced disconnection and/or conflict with

- a family member.

- a girlfriend or boyfriend.

- a friend.

- a teacher or coach.

Describe the feeling of connection. How does your body respond to connection? What kinds of things do you tell yourself when you feel connected?

Describe the feeling of disconnection or loneliness. How does your body respond to loneliness? What kinds of things do you tell yourself when you are lonely?

DEEP LISTENING EXERCISE

Connection in any relationship happens when we make space to hear the other person and when we are heard. This means listening to everything from the mundane details of everyday life to big dreams for the future. Listening—and truly hearing—also allows us to lean into conflict, leading to growth as we learn from moments of disconnection.

For this deep listening exercise, you will need a partner—perhaps your practice partner or a friend or family member. Find a quiet place where you can sit face-to-face. One of you will speak for three minutes, without interruption, about a personal experience of feeling connected or disconnected. Then, you will switch roles and repeat the exercise so that each of you has a chance to share and be heard. When your partner is speaking, try not to get distracted or to ask questions; simply listen as closely as possible.

Before you begin, read and agree on the following guidelines for deep listening:

Listener, here are some key things to know and remember:

- Your role is to be quiet and present.

- Hold in confidence what you hear; trust is crucial.

- You do not need to fix anything or offer advice. Just listen.

- Be curious about and open to what you hear.

- If your mind wanders, gently reengage in listening. Remember: People deserve to be heard.

> You have looked deep into my heart, LORD, and you know all about me. . . . Before I even speak a word, you know what I will say.
>
> **PSALM 139:1, 4 (CEV)**

Speaker, here are some key things to know and remember:

- You are *invited* to share but not forced. If you do not wish to share or if you run out of things to say during your three minutes, you can opt for silence.

- This is a safe place. What you choose to say will be held in confidence.

- Speak from your own experience. Focus on your own thoughts and emotions rather than those of others.

- Respect the experiences of others. Avoid name-calling and debating. Be respectful of your listener as well as of the person about whom you are speaking.

- Sharing your story is a powerful opportunity for healing.[4]

Reflection

- Describe how you felt being the listener.

- Describe how you felt being the speaker.

- How might this deep listening practice help your relationships?

ABIDE

LOVING-KINDNESS MEDITATION

Take some time to practice loving-kindness meditation again, but this time try expanding the practice. You will start in the same way, offering kindness and love to yourself and then extending kindness to someone you love. Then, you will practice sending loving-kindness in the same way to someone with whom you are in conflict. Notice the thoughts and emotions you experience during this meditation without placing pressure or judgment on yourself. If extending loving-kindness to someone with whom you are in conflict becomes uncomfortable, simply return to the practice of extending kindness to someone you love before you conclude the practice.

Listen > *Week 4: Loving-Kindness Meditation 2*

To guide you through this practice, play the audio track "Week 4: Loving-Kindness Meditation 2" at UpperRoomBooks.com/TheAwakenedLife, and follow the instructions.

Prayer

God, help me to be fully present to what you are doing in and through me this week. Amen.

Reflection

- What did you experience during this expanded loving-kindness meditation?
- How did you feel extending loving-kindness to someone with whom you are in conflict or have a difficult relationship?

> Love is had only by loving. If you want love, you must begin by loving—I mean you must want to love.
> **CATHERINE OF SIENA**

ARISE

Today, you expanded beyond self as you began to awaken to your connection with others. You practiced loving-kindness meditation and deep listening techniques. Use these practices this week to begin to strengthen and deepen your connection to others.

HOME PRACTICES FOR WEEK 4

1. Practice the Abide practice (loving-kindness meditation) each day.

2. Keep track of your observations in the practice journal section that follows. For example, on Day 1, enter the date you practiced and the practice: "loving-kindness meditation." Then, record anything you notice about your thoughts, emotions, and physical body. Keep in mind that there is no wrong answer

3. Check in with your partner at least twice this week. You might want to practice together the deep listening exercise and the expanded loving-kindness meditation.

4. Consciously practice deep listening in your everyday conversations this week.

CLOSING BLESSING

We are awakening to abundant life.

We are becoming aware of our worth and belonging.

We are coming alive to our senses, thoughts, and emotions.

We are abiding in the love and grace of God.

We arise now to live a life as connected, whole people.

DAILY PRACTICE JOURNAL

DAY 1

Date: Practice:

What do you notice about your thoughts, emotions, and physical body?

DAY 2

Date: Practice:

What do you notice about your thoughts, emotions, and physical body?

DAY 3

Date: Practice:

What do you notice about your thoughts, emotions, and physical body?

DAY 4

Date: Practice:

What do you notice about your thoughts, emotions, and physical body?

DAY 5

Date: Practice:

What do you notice about your thoughts, emotions, and physical body?

DAY 6

Date: Practice:

What do you notice about your thoughts, emotions, and physical body?

DAY 7

Date: Practice:

What do you notice about your thoughts, emotions, and physical body?

WEEK 5

CONNECTING TO OTHERS

WORKING THROUGH SHAME

AWAKE

Imagine waking up in the morning embraced by divine love. This love provides an unshakable sense of worthiness and belonging. It gives you the courage to know and be known by other people. Imagine being exactly who God created you to be. Authenticity is a gift to others. It enables you to be a great friend because you have empathy and compassion to share. Imagine loving with your whole heart and celebrating with gratitude and joy the knowledge that you are enough. This vision can become a reality in your life. Communion with God and others is possible. This connection is key to the abundant life we have been seeking throughout our weeks together.

> Love from the center of who you are; don't fake it.
>
> ROMANS 12:9-10 (The Message)

AWARE

THE WHY

Dr. Brené Brown is a social work researcher; she collects people's stories and studies them to learn about human behavior. In this talk, she describes her insights into connection and what can help us form or hold us back from meaningful relationships.

Watch > "The Power of Vulnerability"—Brené Brown, TEDx

The TEDx talk is available at UpperRoomBooks.com/TheAwakenedLife or https://www.ted.com/talks/brene_brown_on_vulnerability.

We all have felt shame before. We all have felt as if we aren't good enough, smart enough, or strong enough. Shame is a universal experience. But sadly, it can keep us from being vulnerable and real with others; shame can hold us back from connection.

It is important to note the difference between guilt and shame: Guilt is thinking, *I did something bad*, while shame is thinking, *I am bad*.[1] Guilt helps us realize that we have acted in a way that does not live up to our values and, as a result, have caused hurt. Guilt challenges us to ask for forgiveness and to make a change; it creates an opportunity for growth. Shame, on the other hand, leads us to feel unworthy. If we continually think people will not love the real us, we may begin to feel lonely and isolated. Shame can paralyze us.

> Shame is the intensely painful feeling or experience of believing we are flawed and therefore unworthy of acceptance and belonging.
>
> **BRENÉ BROWN**

ALIVE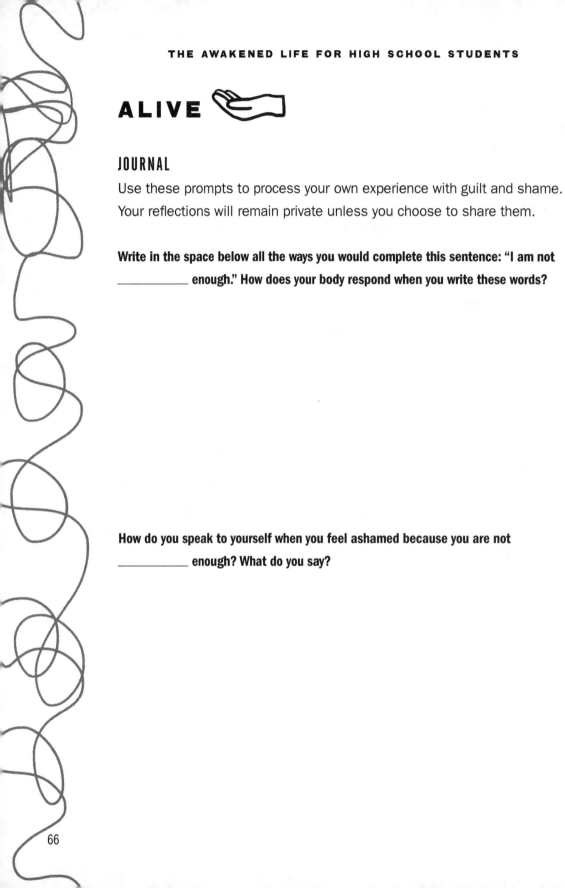

JOURNAL

Use these prompts to process your own experience with guilt and shame. Your reflections will remain private unless you choose to share them.

Write in the space below all the ways you would complete this sentence: "I am not _____ enough." How does your body respond when you write these words?

How do you speak to yourself when you feel ashamed because you are not _____ enough? What do you say?

Young people often experience shame in relation to issues such as body image or showing emotion. What issues have led you to feel shame? What parts of yourself do you want to hide from other people?

If shame were an animal, what would it look like?

Describe a time when you were vulnerable and let people see your imperfections. Who or what gave you the courage to be who you truly are? What happened as a result?

Describe a time when you responded to your own feelings of shame and unworthiness with kindness and compassion. In what ways did that change how you see yourself?

COURAGEOUS CONVERSATIONS

Shame grows in secrecy, silence, and judgment.[2] Courageous conversations are crucial to overcoming shame and allowing for connection with others. They require vulnerability and authenticity. When these conversations happen in a space of deep listening, free of judgment and advice-giving, the sharing of our stories can be powerful and healing.

Instructions

- Write or draw on a piece of paper either a picture of the way your shame looks or feels to you OR one of the ways way you completed this sentence: "I am not _____ enough."

- **Speakers**, share with your partner what you wrote or drew on your paper. Then, if you wish, take a few moments to say anything else you would like to add about your experience with shame.

- **Listeners**, practice deep listening as your partner speaks. Your task is not to "fix" your partner; you cannot erase the experience of shame or minimize its pain. Simply be with the person; offer your listening ear and support. You might respond to your partner with words of affirmation: "You are enough." "You are courageous." "You are loved."

Being vulnerable and naming our shame are acts of courage that can defeat shame. By practicing these courageous conversations with people we trust, we can learn to recognize the spiraling thoughts that lead to shame. With faith and self-compassion, we can begin to break the power of shame in our lives. We do not have to hide in shame. Communion with God and connection with others is not only possible; it also opens the way to the abundant life we are seeking.

> My spirit crushed, I asked, "God, am I not good enough?" As I meditated on Ephesians 2:19, . . . I realized that I do not have to prove myself to others because I am already valued and dearly loved. God's hands made me beautiful. In God's love, I am accepted. In Christ, I am complete.
>
> **APRIL JOY PABUAYA, 25, PHILIPPINES**
> (devozine)

ABIDE

LOVE FEAST

Our spiritual practice for the week is a form of communion—a deep connection with God and with one another. We will celebrate our connection to God and others with a love feast. The love feast is a Christian tradition that recalls the meals Jesus shared with his disciples and honors the community and fellowship we share as the body of Christ. All are welcome at this table.

Originally, this feast was known as the agape meal, echoing the Greek word for "self-giving love" in the New Testament. The setting and symbols of the love feast may remind you of the sacrament of Holy Communion, but these two services are quite distinct. The love feast is a service of sharing food, prayer, hymns, and faith stories. It is a more informal service in which group participation and shared leadership are encouraged. Participants are invited to tell stories of what God is doing in their lives, and youth often are involved in leadership.

Welcome to this table of belonging, acceptance, and love, where we can find courage to know and be known by God and one another. In Christ, God receives us as we are and calls us *enough*—and not *only* enough but *blessed* with God's love and the company of friends.

Instructions

- As we read the love feast liturgy, the Readers and the Leader will read the words in *italics;* the group will read together the words in ***bold italics***.
- When we pass the bread around the table, each person will hold the bread for

> **Dear friends, let's love each other, because love is from God, and everyone who loves is born from God and knows God.**
>
> **1 JOHN 4:7 (CEB)**

the person to the right to take a piece, while offering this blessing: *"[Insert person's name], the gift of life and strength."*

- In the same way, when we pass the pitcher around the table, each person will pour a cup of water for the person to the left, while offering this blessing: *"[Insert person's name], the promise of abundant life."*

- During the meal, everyone will be invited to share stories of the ways they have seen God at work recently—in their lives, in the lives of others in the group, or in the world.

CELEBRATING THE LOVE FEAST

Blessing the Gathering

READER 1: *"How good and pleasant it is when God's people live together in unity!"* (Ps. 133:1, NIV). *Welcome to this meal. We come to share in God's love.*

ALL: *We come to share our food and our lives.*

READER 2: *We come to break bread together and to open ourselves to one another.*

ALL: *We come to express our faith and our thanks.*

READER 3: *We come to taste the living water and to offer our lives in gratitude.*

ALL: *May God bless this food and our fellowship.*

Opening Music

Setting the Table

LEADER: *On this table, in the midst of this community, we place these symbols to remind us that Christ is with us and that his promises are true.*

READER 1: (lighting the candle) *A candle to remind us to walk in the light of Christ's presence. "I am the light of the world. Whoever follows me will never walk in darkness but will have the light of life" (John 8:12).*

READER 2: (placing the basket of bread on the table) *Bread to remind us of Christ's gifts of life and love. "I am the bread of life. . . . The bread that I will give for the life of the world is my flesh" (John 6:48, 51).*

READER 3: (placing the pitcher of water on the table) *Water to remind us that Christ offers us living water and calls us to live life to the fullest. "I came that they may have life, and have it abundantly" (John 10:10).*

ALL: *Christ, we welcome your presence with us. May the food and companionship we share nourish our bodies, hearts, and minds. May our spirits be refreshed as we gather in your presence. Be with us now as you are with all people in all times and places. Amen.*

Serving the Meal

READER 1: *Jesus said, "The bread of God is that which comes down from heaven and gives life to the world" (John 6:33). We take this bread as a symbol of the strength that comes from God, remembering that we can do all things through Christ who strengthens us. (See Philippians 4:13.)*

READER 2: *Jesus said, "Those who drink of the water that I will give them will never be thirsty. The water that I will give will become in them a spring of water gushing up to eternal life." (John 4:14). We receive this water as a symbol of the abundant life Christ offers us.*

READER 3:

Let us pray:

God of Life and Love,

Wake us up to your presence in this moment

so that this everyday meal becomes an eternal feast,

so that our eating and drinking unites us with Christ,

so we know that you live in us and that we live in you,

so that we live in the world, knowing it is yours.

Amen.

Sharing Our Stories

LEADER: *In the past few weeks, how have you seen God working in your life? in the lives of others in our group? in the world around us? How are you experiencing connection with one another and with God?*

Closing Music

Sending Forth with Thanks

ALL: *Loving God,*

We thank you for this meal and for the friends around this table.

In the sharing of your life-giving bread and your living water,

    may we come to know communion with you and one another.

Move in us so that we are awake in each moment

    to experience the abundant life you offer.

Make us aware of our guilt and shame,

    and compassionately transform us with grace.

Bring us to life with your Spirit

   so that we can listen deeply and offer empathy to others.

Abide in us so that we will have strength and peace

   to be powerful forces of love in the world.

Allow us to arise in the grace of your love,

   fully alive to our purpose and grounded in eternal hope.

Through this shared meal with a community that is growing in love,

   help us to know our worth and to feel in our souls that we truly belong.

Thank you for your incredible invitation to experience your love and grace.

We praise you and look forward to sharing with all your people

   your promise of abundant life in Christ. Amen.

Reflection

Take a few moments to reflect on your experience of the love feast. How did you feel about participating in this agape meal immediately following your conversations about shame? What do you notice about your thoughts, emotions, and physical body after this meal? Write or draw anything that comes to mind.

ARISE

Today, you learned about overcoming shame and experiencing connection and communion. Use the courageous conversations and loving-kindness meditation to continue overcoming shame and seeking connection to yourself, God, and others.

HOME PRACTICES FOR WEEK 5

1. Continue to practice loving-kindness meditation each day.

2. Have a courageous conversation about shame with a friend or family member this week. Then, reread the Abide section and record any further insights you have about the love feast.

3. Keep track of your observations in the practice journal area that follows. For example, on Day 1, enter the date you practiced and the practice: "loving-kindness meditation." Then, record anything you notice about your thoughts, emotions, and physical body. Keep in mind that there is no wrong answer.

4. Check in with your practice partner at least twice this week. Talk about the courageous conversations you had in this session and about the experience of letting go of the thoughts that lead to shame.

CLOSING BLESSING

We are awakening to abundant life.

We are becoming aware of our worth and belonging.

We are becoming alive to our senses, thoughts, and emotions.

We are abiding in the love and grace of God.

We arise now to live a life as connected, whole people.

DAILY PRACTICE JOURNAL

DAY 1

Date: Practice:

What do you notice about your thoughts, emotions, and physical body?

DAY 2

Date: Practice:

What do you notice about your thoughts, emotions, and physical body?

DAY 3

Date: Practice:

What do you notice about your thoughts, emotions, and physical body?

DAY 4

Date: Practice:

What do you notice about your thoughts, emotions, and physical body?

DAY 5

Date: Practice:

What do you notice about your thoughts, emotions, and physical body?

DAY 6

Date: Practice:

What do you notice about your thoughts, emotions, and physical body?

DAY 7

Date: Practice:

What do you notice about your thoughts, emotions, and physical body?

DAY 6

Date: Practice:

What do you notice about your thoughts, emotions, and physical body?

DAY 7

Date: Practice:

What do you notice about your thoughts, emotions, and physical body?

WEEK 6

CONNECTING TO CREATION

EXPERIENCING AWE OF NATURE

AWAKE 👁

Do you remember the last time you sat appreciating the rustling of green leaves against an indigo sky? The sun warmed you, and the wind caressed your face. Maybe on another day you went outside after a rain, smelled the clean air, and counted the earthworms on the sidewalk. A puddle of water called to you to jump and splash. The wet soil tempted you to squish together a mud pie with your bare hands. What about an evening outside when you glimpsed the first star appearing at dusk and you waited for the flash of a firefly to chase? Even better, you stayed still so the fireflies came close, and you were surrounded by their light under the glow of starlight. These moments are gifts from our Creator God.

In the beginning, God placed the earth neither too far nor too close to the sun to perfectly sustain life. Then, God created us along with plants and animals and gave us the role of gardener, steward of the planet. For some, this stewardship means digging in the earth, planting the seeds, and nurturing the growth of food and flowers. For all, it means connecting to the seasons, praying for the farmers, conserving resources, and holding awe for the cycle of life. Yet, with the convenience of grocery stores and modern transportation, we are more disconnected from how our food is raised. In our busyness, we consume the earth's resources with little appreciation. We go from our homes to our cars to our schools with our earbuds in, without noticing the sun, the trees, the clouds, or the bird's chirp of greeting. Connecting to nature is another key to wholeness.

One night during our summer vacation, my family decided to go out on the beach to look at the stars. What I saw that night changed my life forever. An ocean of stars—more than I had ever seen—illuminated the darkness. What a perfect way to reveal to us how great our God is!

EVAN KOZAK, 18, GEORGIA
(devozine)

Reflection

- Describe a time when you felt connected to nature or a moment in nature that woke you up to something extraordinary.

AWARE

THE WHY

Scientific research shows time outdoors has a positive impact on our physical, emotional, mental, and spiritual health. Spending time in nature may help to address specific problems such as depression and anxiety. Research in *Environmental Health Perspectives* tells us this: "Contact with nature offers promise both as prevention and as treatment across the life course."[1] Yet, even though we hear reports about the importance of time in nature, the time we spend outside is not increasing. Media consumption, however, *is* on the rise; studies indicate that teens spend an average of nine hours a day plugged in.[2] Research demonstrates that visiting parks, camping, hunting, fishing, and children playing outdoors have all declined substantially over recent decades.[3]

JOURNAL

Describe the most recent time you spent outside. Where were you? What could you see, hear, smell, taste, and touch?

Where is your favorite place to go outside? What do you like about this place? How do you feel when you are there?

Describe a time when you experienced a deep sense of connection with God in the natural world. How and where did you experience this connection?

What keeps you from being outside more often? What do you think keeps other people inside?

ALIVE

PRAYER WALK

Head outdoors, and take a prayer walk. Practice gratitude as you walk. Be thankful for all you observe in the natural world. The prayer walk will last fifteen minutes. Refrain from looking at your phone or other screens during this time.

Instructions

1. Set a timer for fifteen minutes on your phone, but then put it away.

2. Practice paying attention and focusing on the natural world.

3. If your mind wanders, bring yourself gently back into focus without judgment.

4. Silently express gratitude for what you see, hear, smell, and touch.

5. Pray for connection with and appreciation for the world around you.

6. Pray that all the living things that you encounter will experience abundant life.

7. If the weather is nice, you might take off your shoes. Feel grounded in the earth that solidly supports you.

> **Walking mindfully on the earth, we are nourished by the trees, the bushes, the flowers, and the sunshine. Touching the earth is a very deep practice that can restore our peace and our joy.**
>
> **THICH NHAT HANH**

8. Finally, find a comfortable place. Pick one living organism you find there (for example, a leaf, a blade of grass, a bug, or tree bark). Spend your last five minutes looking at it with a loving gaze. Open yourself to what God is revealing to you through this small part of creation.

Reflection

- What did you notice during your prayer walk? What stood out to you? What did you see, hear, smell, or touch?

- What happened in your body as you experienced the outdoors?

- How did you feel before you started the walk? How do you feel now?

- What words come to mind when you think about your prayer walk experience? Write two or three of those words in the blank circle here:

ABIDE

CENTERING PRAYER

The practice of Centering Prayer is an invitation to focus on God's presence in and around you. Take some time with this practice to consider your awe of God's creation.

Instructions

1. Pick a sacred word to use during your prayer time to help you focus on God. You might use one of the words you wrote after the prayer walk. Or you might choose another sacred word, such as *Creator, awe, connected, nature,* or *beauty.*

2. Sit comfortably in silence with your eyes closed and your mind open to God.

3. When your mind begins to wander and thoughts begin to form, silently repeat your sacred word and gently return to focusing on God's presence around you and within you.

4. When the Centering Prayer time is over, before you open your eyes, take a few moments to observe any thoughts or emotions you experienced or anything you sensed in your body during the prayer.

Prayer

God, help me stay connected to my sense of awe for creation. Amen.

I hear God's voice in the ocean waves rolling onto the sand. I smell God's blessings in the rich soil while hiking in the woods. I see God's gentle spirit in the deer that graze among the trees. The glory of the Lord is all around us. Let's make sure we never stop looking.

SARA ARMSTRONG, 17, GEORGIA
(devozine)

ARISE

Today, you learned about the power of connecting with nature. Use the home practices to continue increasing your awareness of the natural environment and to notice how spending time in creation affects your body, mind, and spirit.

HOME PRACTICES FOR WEEK 6

1. Practice Centering Prayer each day for at least three minutes. You can use the same sacred word you used today or choose a new word each day.

2. Keep track of your observations in the practice journal area that follows. For example, on Day 1, enter the date you practiced and the practice: "Centering Prayer." Then, record anything you notice about your thoughts, emotions, and physical body. Keep in mind that there is no wrong answer.

3. Get outside! Take a prayer walk in your neighborhood at least twice this week. If weather keeps you inside, try a tech fast. Spend at least an hour away from your phone and other screens.

4. Check in with your practice partner at least twice this week. You might want to take a silent prayer walk together and then talk about how you felt during that experience.

CLOSING BLESSING

We are awakening to abundant life.

We are becoming aware of our worth and belonging.

We are becoming alive to our senses, thoughts, and emotions.

We are abiding in the love and grace of God.

We arise now to live a life as connected, whole people.

DAILY PRACTICE JOURNAL

DAY 1

Date: Practice:

What do you notice about your thoughts, emotions, and physical body?

DAY 2

Date: Practice:

What do you notice about your thoughts, emotions, and physical body?

DAY 3

Date: Practice:

What do you notice about your thoughts, emotions, and physical body?

DAY 4

Date: Practice:

What do you notice about your thoughts, emotions, and physical body?

DAY 5

Date: Practice:

What do you notice about your thoughts, emotions, and physical body?

DAY 6

Date: Practice:

What do you notice about your thoughts, emotions, and physical body?

DAY 7

Date: Practice:

What do you notice about your thoughts, emotions, and physical body?

"But ask the animals, and they will
teach you; the birds of the air, and they
will tell you; ask the plants of the earth, and they will
teach you; and the fish of the sea will declare to you.
Who among all these does not know that the hand of
the Lᴏʀᴅ has done this? In his hand is the
life of every living thing and the breath of
every human being."

JOB 12:7-10

WEEK 7

CONNECTING TO CREATION

SHARING A MEAL OF INTENTION

AWAKE

For weeks, we have been working to quiet our minds and to limit distractions so that we are able to experience God through our connections with self, others, and nature. The meal we are going to share today brings all of our work together. Making, preparing, and sharing food provides an opportunity to experience the presence of God.

Meals give us a glimpse of heaven. Creation offers us nourishment, friends bless us with their presence, we share ourselves in conversation, and God binds us all together in love.

> You are all my relations, my relatives, without whom I would not live.
> **LAKOTA SIOUX PRAYER**

The shared meal is important throughout different cultures. The Lakota Sioux people have a prayer, "Mitakuye Oyasin," that celebrates God's creation through our connection to minerals, plants, animals, humans, and Spirit. Our indigenous brothers and sisters remind us that when the earth thrives, we thrive, and that when the earth hurts, so do we.

Meals are experiences of radical hospitality and love in the Judeo-Christian faith tradition. At a meal, care is extended for all who join around the table. Jesus invited himself to a greedy tax collector's house and restored that man to his community. (See Luke 19:1–10.) At a prestigious dinner party, Jesus allowed a "sinful woman" to anoint his feet with oil and then blessed her with healing and hope. (See Luke 7:36-37.) Another time, when thousands were gathered for Jesus' teachings, the disciples wanted Jesus to send the people away to feed themselves at mealtime. Yet, Jesus invited a miraculous sharing, and all were fed to the point of full bellies and souls. (See Mark 6:30-44.) Powerful things happen at meals. Lives are shared and connected by the simple yet profound act of breaking bread together as we open ourselves to God's possibilities for our lives.

AWARE

THE WHY

In our fast-food culture, the preparing and sharing of meals often goes missing. A 2018 survey revealed that almost one in three Americans "can't get through a meal without being on their phones."[1] Over 70 percent of the two thousand people surveyed reported that they often watch TV while eating.[2] These habits lead to disconnection from the people with whom we are eating as well as disconnection from our food. While distracted by their phones, people are more likely to chew less and to eat more. Eating on the go rather than around a table distances us from the fellowship involved in preparing and eating a meal. It also decreases our knowledge of and gratitude for the efforts of all who made that meal possible. To get the physical, emotional, and spiritual health benefits of shared meals, three things are crucial: putting down our phones, engaging in conversation, and being grateful for the meal in front of us.

> To be well-fed,
> we need to pay attention
> to the ways we can nourish
> ourselves—body and soul.
> **ANNA SWAIN, 18, NEW MEXICO**
> (devozine)

93

ALIVE

To truly be grateful for the meal you are about to share, consider its origins. Take some time to think about the people involved and processes required to grow, produce, and transport the various ingredients for this meal. Be grateful for those who helped to get this food to you, and be aware of how your food's production affects the earth.

GROUP RESEARCH

1. Where was this ingredient likely grown? Is it in season in our region right now?

2. What went into the growing and/or making of this ingredient?

3. What people may have been involved in growing or making this ingredient and in getting it to our table? Were any of these people working under oppressive conditions?

4. How was the earth positively and negatively affected by the growth or production of this ingredient? How eco-friendly were the processes or chemicals involved in providing us with this part of our meal?

5. What nutritional value does this ingredient offer our bodies? Why is that information relevant to an awakened life?

6. What unanswered questions do you have?

ABIDE

MINDFUL EATING: SHARING A MEAL OF INTENTION

This week's practice is mindful eating. This practice is an effort to savor our food and to express gratitude. As we share this meal of intention, these instructions and prompts will help us to get the most out of the experience.

Instructions

- Put away all screens so you can be fully present during the meal.
- Practice being silent for the first five or ten minutes of the meal.
- Consider what you smell, feel, taste, and experience with each bite.
- Try to chew each bite thirty times.
- Think back to your research. What people were involved and what processes went into the making of this food?
- Take a moment to be thankful for each step of this process and all the people and natural resources needed to nourish your body in this moment.

Meal Conversation Starters

After the time of silence, continue the meal as you share together in a conversation about the following questions:

- How did you feel while eating in silence without your phone and intentionally staying present to your eating experience?
- How did your research about the ingredients and the people who grew and prepared them affect your eating experience?
- How did this meal compare to other meals you eat at home or at school?

> The dream of God is that all creation will live together in peace and harmony and fulfillment. All parts of creation.
> **VERNA DOZIER**

- What are your meal practices at home? Does your family eat together, or does everyone eat separately?

- What kind of conversations do you have during meals at school?

- What practices could you incorporate into your life to show gratitude for the food you eat?

The kitchen is an absolute mess, but my heart is full of joy. Dust and flour dance together in the sunlight streaming through the window. The hearty smells of pasta and oregano waft through the air. I cradle a cool glass of iced tea in my hands. It's Sunday afternoon, and I am with friends. We are enjoying lunch and the chance to be together. . . . We share joys, burdens, tears, prayers, and praises; we give thanks for the small community we have built.

SALINA MCGINNISS, PENNSYLVANIA (devozine)

ARISE

Today, you awakened to experiencing God through your connections with self, others, and creation in the sharing of a meal. Use the home practices to help you stay awake to this interconnectedness.

HOME PRACTICES FOR WEEK 7

1. Practice mindful eating during one meal each day. Try adding more meals so that mindful eating gradually becomes a regular practice.

2. Keep track of your observations in the practice journal area that follows. For example, on Day 1, enter the date you practiced and the practice: "mindful eating." Then, record anything you notice about your thoughts, emotions, and physical body. Keep in mind that there is no wrong answer.

3. Check in with your practice partner at least twice this week. Share a meal together if you can.

CLOSING BLESSING

We are awakening to abundant life.

We are becoming aware of our worth and belonging.

We are coming alive to our senses, thoughts, and emotions.

We are abiding in the love and grace of God.

We arise now to live a life as connected, whole people.

DAILY PRACTICE JOURNAL

DAY 1

Date: Practice:

What do you notice about your thoughts, emotions, and physical body?

DAY 2

Date: Practice:

What do you notice about your thoughts, emotions, and physical body?

DAY 3

Date: Practice:

What do you notice about your thoughts, emotions, and physical body?

DAY 4

Date: Practice:

What do you notice about your thoughts, emotions, and physical body?

DAY 5

Date: Practice:

What do you notice about your thoughts, emotions, and physical body?

DAY 6

Date: Practice:

What do you notice about your thoughts, emotions, and physical body?

DAY 7

Date: Practice:

What do you notice about your thoughts, emotions, and physical body?

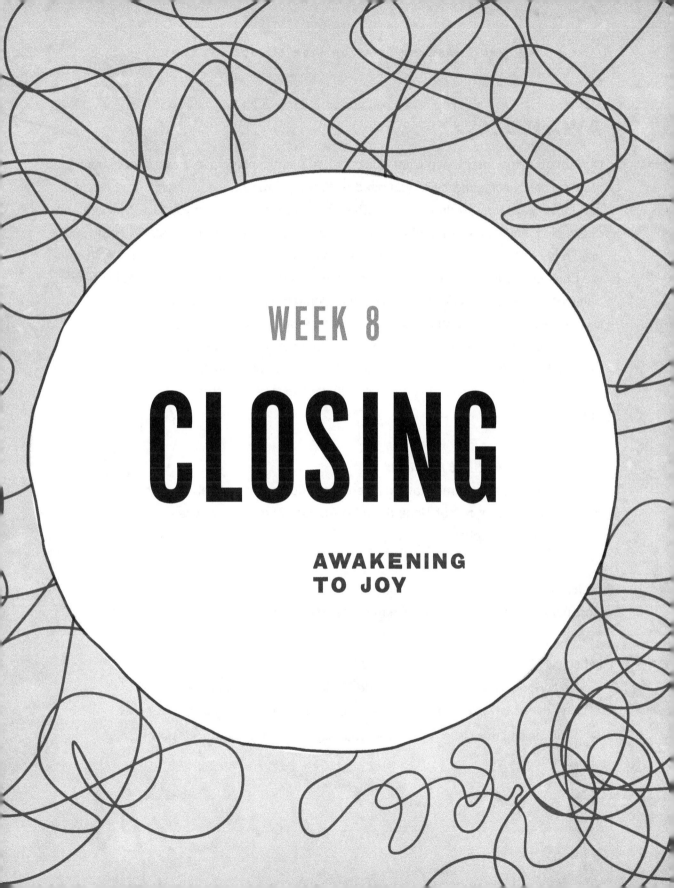

WEEK 8

CLOSING

AWAKENING TO JOY

AWAKE

Our work together over these eight weeks is just the beginning of an awakened, abundant life. You are building the skills you need to be fully awake to your feelings and thoughts and to the ways they live in your body. This self-awareness will help you face criticism and disappointment with a sense of your own worth. This sense of worthiness will help you to build a life of connection, and these connections will strengthen you to face challenges. In the Christian tradition, connection to the Spirit of God allows for a life of "love, joy, peace, patience, kindness, goodness, faithfulness, gentleness, and self-control" (Gal. 5:22-23, CEB). A life that cultivates these qualities can persevere through struggles.

One way we can begin to awaken to joy is to practice gratitude. Often, we forget—or simply take for granted—all the things in our lives that are cause for thankfulness. Being aware of these things takes some practice.

> The joy of the LORD is your strength.
> NEHEMIAH 8:10

Listen > *Week 8: Gratitude Meditation*

To practice the gratitude meditation, listen to the audio track "Week 8: Gratitude Meditation" at UpperRoomBooks.com/TheAwakenedLife, and follow the instructions.

Prayer

God, help me continue to be awake to your presence in all aspects of my life. Amen.

Reflection

- How did you feel as you participated in the gratitude meditation?
- Think back to the first time you practiced meditation in Week 1 (the awareness meditation). How was your experience today similar? How was it different?

AWARE

Spiritual disciplines and mindfulness can help to reduce stress. All the mindful, meditative, and spiritual practices you have experienced during our time together help to train your mind to tolerate negativity, boredom, and anxiety. These practices offer calm in the storms of life by connecting you to God through your relationships with self, others, and nature.

Reflection

- After all these weeks, what does "awakened life" mean to you now?

ALIVE

GROUP GRATITUDE EXERCISE

Joy is discovered through gratitude. One great source of joy is the time we have had together as a group. Communicating these feelings of gratitude is a powerful way to express appreciation and love for one another. In this exercise, you will have the opportunity to tell the members of your group how they have helped or inspired you over the last eight weeks.

> When stress overwhelms us, we want relief. But being still is probably the last remedy we consider. Yet something happens when we stop, sit down, take a deep breath, and say, "God, I am here."
>
> **ROBERT BRANDHORST, NEW JERSEY**
> **(devozine)**

JOURNAL

What are some things people said to you during the group gratitude exercise that you would like to remember? What about those comments was meaningful or challenged you to grow?

What insights have you discovered about yourself during these eight weeks? In what ways have you changed? Complete the blanks in this sentence: "Seven weeks ago, I was _____. Now I am _____."

What aspect of this study are you most thankful for? What else in your life are you thankful for? How will you express your gratitude?

Which practices do you plan to continue after this session? Why have you chosen these practices? How are they helpful to you?

ABIDE

DAILY EXAMEN

Ignatius of Loyola, a Christian leader of the sixteenth century, created the Daily Examen. An awareness and gratitude prayer, the Daily Examen can be used to reflect on our day. This practice has been passed down through Christian generations as a way to give God our attention, to listen for God's direction, and to be thankful for all the moments in our lives.

> We need resilience and hope and a spirit that can carry us through the doubt and fear. We need to believe that we can effect change if we want to live and love with our whole hearts.
>
> **BRENÉ BROWN**

Instructions

You might use all of these steps or choose a few to focus on more intentionally during your prayer time.

1. **Invite God's Presence**: Take a few moments to invite the Holy Spirit to help you see how God was active and working in and through you during the day.

2. **Practice Gratitude**: As you replay your day in your mind, what moments are you particularly thankful for and why?

3. **Consider Your Emotions**: What emotions did you experience today? What can they teach you about yourself?

4. **Pick a Moment**: Choose a scene from your day, and pray about it with extra focus. Was there a moment in which you regretted your words, actions, or thoughts? Do you need to extend compassion to yourself or to someone else? Was there a moment that was life-giving? What does it reveal about what is truly important to you?

5. **Look Forward**: What is coming up in your life? In what areas of your life do you want to ask God for strength, direction, connection, or hope?

Reflection

You can use this space that follows to record any thoughts, feelings, moments of gratitude, or clarity from God about your life that you experience as you practice.

Rejoice always,
pray without ceasing, give
thanks in all circumstances;
for this is the will of God
in Christ Jesus for you.

1 THESSALONIANS 5:16-18

ARISE

Today is the last day of this study but only the beginning of an awakened life. May you carry all the practices with you and use them often so that they can support you when the struggles of life come. These mindfulness and spiritual practices will help you deepen your connection to God, to yourself, to others, and to all of creation. Being able to draw upon these practices, in good times and bad, will enable you to experience profound peace and joy.

HOME PRACTICES FOR WEEK 8 AND BEYOND

1. Practice being awake every day with the mindfulness and spiritual exercises you have learned in this group. These exercises will keep you connected to God, yourself, others, and nature.

2. Select a sketchpad or notebook to use as a daily practice journal, and continue to draw or write about the ways your practice affects your body, mind, and spirit. Wholeness is at your fingertips.

3. Treat yourself gently with self-compassion, and give thanks for God's many blessings.

4. Stay in communication with your practice partner and with others in the group.

CLOSING BLESSING

We are awakening to abundant life.

We are becoming aware of our worth and belonging.

We are becoming alive to our senses, thoughts, and emotions.

We are abiding in the love and grace of God.

We arise now to live a life as connected, whole people.

NOTES

Week 1—Introduction to the Awakened Life

1. "Adolescent Mental Health Basics," U.S. Department of Health and Human Services, February 25, 2019, https://www.hhs.gov/ash/oah/adolescent-development/mental-health/adolescent-mental-health-basics/index.html.
2. "Stress Management and Teens," American Academy of Child and Adolescent Psychiatry, January 2019, https://www.aacap.org/AACAP/Families_and_Youth/Facts_for_Families/FFF-Guide/Helping-Teenagers-With-Stress-066.aspx.
3. Hafiz and Daniel Ladinsky, "Awake Awhile," *I Heard GOD Laughing: Poems of Hope and Joy, Renderings of Hafiz by Daniel Ladinsky* (New York: Penguin, 1996, 2006), 38.
4. John O'Donohue, "The Question Holds the Lantern," *The Sun*, November 2009, http://www.thesunmagazine.org/issues/407/the-question-holds-the-lantern.

Week 2—Connecting to Self: Noticing Thoughts

1. Steve Bradt, "Wandering Mind Not a Happy Mind," *The Harvard Gazette*, November 11, 2010, https://news.harvard.edu/gazette/story/2010/11/wandering-mind-not-a-happy-mind/.
2. Adapted from Bob Stahl and Elisha Goldstein, *A Mindfulness-Based Stress Reduction Workbook* (Oakland, CA: New Harbinger Publications, 2010), 55–56. Stahl and Goldstein's list of negative thought patterns includes catastrophizing, mind-reading, the "shoulds," and blaming, among others.
3. Kristin Neff, quoted in Kristin Wong, "Why Self-Compassion Beats Self-Confidence," *The New York Times*, December 28, 2017, https://www.nytimes.com/2017/12/28/smarter-living/why-self-compassion-beats-self-confidence.html.
4. Neff, quoted in Wong, "Why Self-Compassion Beats Self-Confidence."

Week 3—Connecting to Self: Being Present in the Body

1. Deborah J. Cohan, "Cell Phones and College Students," *Psychology Today,* April 30, 2016, https://www.psychologytoday.com/us/blog/social-lights/201604/cell-phones-and-college-students.

Week 4—Connecting to Others: Working Through Loneliness

1. Claudia Hammond, "The Surprising Truth About Loneliness," *BBC Future*, September 30, 2018, https://www.bbc.com/future/article/20180928-the-surprising-truth-about-loneliness

2. Arash Emamzadeh, "Loneliness and Media Usage: A Study of 8 Million Americans," *Psychology Today*, August 22, 2019, https://www.psychologytoday.com/us/blog/finding-new-home/2019 08/loneliness-and-media-usage-study-8-million-americans.

3. Anna Haensch, "When Choirs Sing, Many Hearts Beat as One," NPR, July 10, 2013, https://www.npr.org/sections/health-shots/2013/07/09/200390454/when-choirs-sing-many-hearts-beat-as-one.

4. Guidelines for speakers and listeners are adapted from Parker Palmer's Circle of Trust Touchstones. These Touchstones can be found online at www.couragerenewal.org/touchstones or in Palmer, *A Hidden Wholeness: The Journey Toward an Undivided Life* (San Francisco: Jossey-Bass, 2004), 217–18.

Week 5—Connecting to Others: Working Through Shame

1. Brené Brown, *Daring Greatly: How the Courage to Be Vulnerable Transforms the Way We Live, Love, Parent, and Lead* (New York: Penguin, 2012), 71.

2. Brown, "Listening to Shame," filmed March 2012, TED video, 20:23, https://www.ted.com/talks/brene_brown_listening_to_shame.

Week 6—Connecting to Creation: Experiencing Awe of Nature

1. Howard Frumkin et al., "Nature Contact and Human Health: A Research Agenda," *Environmental Health Perspectives* 125, no. 7 (July 2017), https://ehp.niehs.nih.gov/doi/10.1289/EHP1663.

2. Hayley Tsukayama, "Teens Spend Nearly Nine Hours Every Day Consuming Media," *The Washington Post*, November 2, 2015, https://www.washingtonpost.com/news/the-switch/wp/2015/11/03/teens-spend-nearly-nine-hours-every-day-consuming-media/

3. Frumkin et al., "Nature Contact and Human Health."

Week 7—Connecting to Creation: Sharing a Meal of Intention

1. Lily Rose, "1 in 3 Americans Can't Eat a Meal Without Being on Their Phone," *Orlando Sentinel*, January 24, 2018, http://www.orlandosentinel.com/features/food/sns-dailymeal-1867994-eat-americans-cant-eat-without-being-on-their-phones-20180124-story.html.

2. Rose, "1 in 3 Americans."

Week 8—Closing: Awakening to Joy

1. Adapted from "How Can I Pray?" Loyola Press, IgnatianSpirituality.com, accessed January 14, 2019, https://www.ignatianspirituality.com/ignatian-prayer/the-examen/how-can-i-pray.

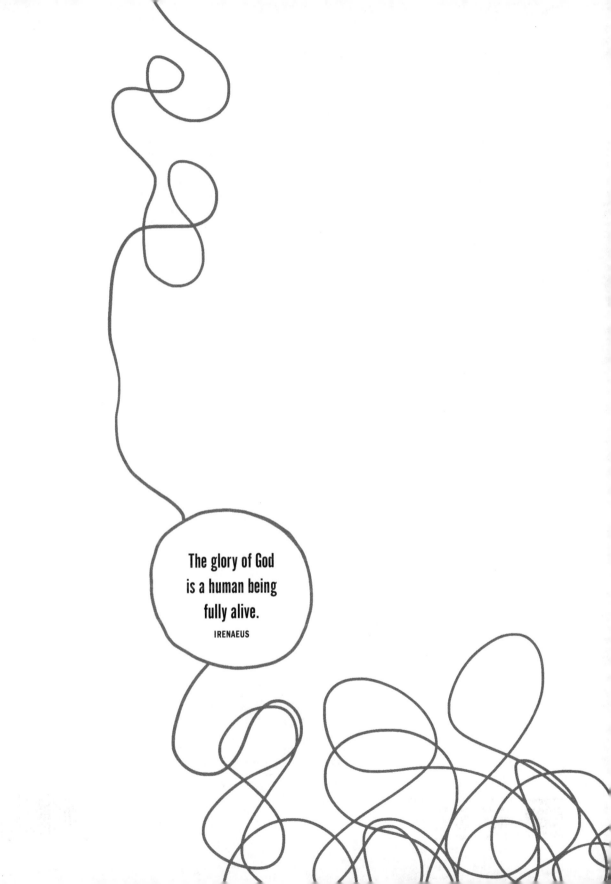

The glory of God
is a human being
fully alive.
IRENAEUS

CPSIA information can be obtained
at www.ICGtesting.com
Printed in the USA
LVHW100713030720
659548LV00006B/141

9 780835 819398